The Affi

MW00977234

The Affirmative Action Dilemma

Kirklin R. Anglin

ISBN : 1-4196-0996-3

To order additional copies, please contact us.
BookSurge, LLC
www.booksurge.com
1-866-308-6235
orders@booksurge.com

The Affirmative Action Dilemma

TABLE OF CONTENTS

As in every undertaking there are those who play a significant role in moving visions from dreams to reality. I take this opportunity to express thanks to my friend of twenty-three years, pastor Lawrence Jackson I, for encouraging me to continue with my writing; my sister Cheryl for helping with the proof reading; my brother David and my mother Lula for their enormous support through some challenging situations. Thanks to both my father and mother for passing on the values and principles that serve to enhance the worth of one's life. My greatest appreciation to my brothers: Will, Anane and Lance and to my sister Lynette for their support over the years. To my darling wife Yolanda, who has supported my every effort during ten years of marriage and who also read every little change I made. Thanks for reading through revision after revision; you are appreciated more and more. To Shea, Nikki and Lacey, my daughters, you are all greatly loved. Shea, I commend and congratulate you for exercising the discipline and determination necessary to earn your degree at LSU - - great job! To my favorite son, Jeremiah, and my granddaughter Imani, may you both discover and fulfill God's purpose for your lives. Finally, all praises and thanks to God for blessing me with a hunger and thirst for truth and for granting a measure of insight into the inexhaustible principles found in the Scriptures.

-- Kirklin R. Anglin

Chapter 1

Thirsting for Truth

Blessed are they who do hunger and thirst after righteousness; for they shall be filled. - Matthew 5:6

To attempt discussing a subject that evokes such strong and varied feelings among so many people from all avenues of life demands an open mind as well as an open heart. The ability to exercise objectivity seems a rare quality these days, but an indispensable one if we are to extract truth amidst generations of tradition and perception. Rare indeed is the occasion to find one who values the discovery of truth, and truth alone, above all else... truth above public opinion, reputation, image, party politics and the like. Only when we are sincerely in pursuit of the truth and preoccupied with obtaining it can we properly identify it once it presents itself. The biblical account of Cornelius, found in Acts chapter 10, provides an excellent example of how God moves in the life of one who has both a longing for truth and a desire to do that which is right.

There was a certain man in Caesarea called Cornelius, a centurion of the band called the Italian band, A devout man,

and one that feared God with all his house, who gave alms to the people, and prayed to God always (Acts 10:1,2).

This is a situation where Cornelius did the best he could with the insight and understanding that he possessed. He was devout, gave alms (donations to the less fortunate) and, like Daniel of the Old Testament, he was consistent in his prayer life. However, even the sum of all of these qualities coupled with sincerity left Cornelius on a platform that was yet inadequate before God. What we should find most striking in this scenario is that God responds neither to the nobility of Cornelius' deeds nor their inadequacy, but rather to Cornelius' character and his spirit. It is here that we find the essence of the man, a centurion, saturated with a longing to do that which was right in the eyes of the Lord. The word of God is quite clear in its teaching that God is not moved so much by what we do, as He is the reason why we do what we do. The following Scriptures can illustrate this:

And he said unto him, Thy prayers and thine alms are come up for a memorial before God (Acts 10:4).

And Abel, he also brought of the firstlings of his flock and of the fat thereof. And the Lord had respect unto Abel and unto his offering (Genesis 4:4).

Take a close look at the verses above. God did not respond to Cornelius' alms and his prayers nor did He give recognition to Abel's offering and then to Abel. The response is directed firstly to that which emanates from the heart and secondly to those deeds which are a result of that which is borne in the heart. God deals with the intangible and the invisible before acknowledging those things that are readily noted by the physical senses.

...for the Lord seeth not as man seeth; for man looketh on the outward appearance, but the Lord looketh on the heart (1 Samuel 16:7).

Thus, in the Cornelius account we find God at work bringing a heavenly vision to a Roman centurion and instructing him to send for a Jew, Simon Peter, to tell him what it is that he ought to do (Acts 10:3-6). Blessed are they who do hunger and thirst after righteousness, for then and only then will they meet Him who is the bread of life and find themselves drinking from the thirst quenching water of life.

Now picture for a moment if you will a pilgrim traveling across the desert. The desert heat has parched his lips and the beaming rays of the sun have thoroughly burned his skin. His throat is dry from the heat of the desert's arid air and irritated by the dust of the desert's sand. What does he want? What does this pilgrim crave? Lips parched, skin burned, throat dry, sore, and irritated by the dusty grit of the arid hot desert sand. What is the single yearning of his soul -- *only water* -- nothing but *water*, got to have some *waaaaa-ter*!

While there are many who hunger and long for truth like the desert traveler panting for water, there are still others who when confronted by the truth can never embrace it. These are they who for so long have verbalized a position contrary to the truth, that the truth would not be received even if delivered to their front door by deity. To now embrace a point of view that might (1) resemble acceptance of a position that was formerly declared totally incomprehensible, (2) appear to communicate a change in sentiment or (3) be looked upon, as recanting of their former philosophical predisposition, would be unthinkable. After all, what would that do to their image, their reputation, their ego or pride, and of course their loyal devotees if any?

Certainly nothing could be more important than these! Not to mention the thought of becoming something of a public spectacle. The dominant focus in most instances for those who find themselves confronting this type of dilemma is, "me, myself and I." It's what the late Dr. J. Vernon Magee, a noted Bible scholar, would probably call a bad case of perpendicular I-E-TUS. It's another way of saying that someone is overly consumed with self. Those who think this way give testimony that they are not truly aware of, nor are they in search of the greater meaning of this journey through the desert of life. Protecting their egos and their reputations, they destine themselves to sink deeper and deeper into a state of self-deception fueled by willful ignorance. Never will they experience fulfillment, for as the Word testifies, it comes only as a by-product of the truth. *"Blessed are they who do hunger and thirst after righteousness for they shall be filled."* Scarce indeed are those who will sacrifice ego, image, political advantage and following, in favor of the truth. Therefore, the greatest task at hand as we encroach upon our subject is one of self-evaluation. *"To thine own self be true, and it must follow as the night the day, Thou canst not then be false to any man."* - - William Shakespeare.

Without a doubt, the subject of Affirmative Action is not only extremely controversial but also unquestionably misunderstood, which no doubt contributes considerably to the subject's ongoing controversy. It is a wonder that no one has said, "There are three things I don't discuss: religion, politics and Affirmative Action." That being said let me acknowledge that there is considerable potential for tension and frustration associated with prolonged deliberations on a topic such as this one. Therefore, those who would continue reading must possess the ability to objectively and rationally assess viewpoints that may differ from their own, in spite of the emotional charge of personal convictions. Thus, I challenge you to self-evaluation as you ponder the question, "Am I thirsty for *Truth and Justice?*" It is my hope that your answer is nothing other than a resounding, "*Yes!*"

Chapter 2

At The Heart Of The Controversy

A good man out of the good treasure of the heart bringeth forth good things, and an evil man out of the evil treasure bringeth forth evil things. ~ Matthew 12:35

When you give close attention to the Affirmative Action controversy it should become rather clear that many of the terms or phrases used to reference Affirmative Action are not only packed with emotion but are also very divisive. Consider for example: (1) preferential treatment, (2) reverse discrimination, and (3) hiring unqualified minorities. These expressions voice the sentiments that are at the very core of the debate and generate an atmosphere of cyclic resentment. There is resentment by whites, due to the belief that they are treated unjustly for crimes that their ancestors or forefathers committed. This bitterness is fed by the idea that the efforts to help minorities actually embrace the very practices which they are attempting to combat. Then on the other hand, resentment by Blacks who perceive a persistent reluctance on the part of society to: (1) acknowledge the injustices of the past without attempts at justification, (2) adequately make amends for the injustices of the past and (3) acknowledge the racist and unjust practices that are still realities of the present. Some would suggest that the eradication of slavery and the impact of the Civil Rights movement have brought us to an enlightened era, free of racial woes and injustice, a *pseudoutopia* if you will. However, though we may agree that justice is blind we must forever be painfully aware that the administrators of justice are not. Subsequently they are subject to the imperfections of human nature among which we find the lingering poison of prejudice.

As we approach our discussion, it behooves us to recognize some of the dominant perceptions within the context of this subject. Furthermore, if we would move forward in understanding, we are confronted with the awesome task of discerning what is perception versus what is true. However, let it be understood that perception is the power that directly affects what one holds to as truth or falsehood. But what exactly is perception? Some might say that it is merely opinion, but it is considerably more complex than mere opinion. It involves the conclusions we come to about some subject or situation based on observation and the analysis of information related to the issue being contemplated. The conclusions we reach are inextricably tied to how we process the information we have. Our perceptions are established by the judgments we make from the particles of data we take in and inevitably piece together in what we believe to be a logical fashion. The conclusions we come to ultimately become part of our belief system, affecting how we define what we believe to be true. Furthermore, while our perceptions are usually based on a multitude of factors, these factors when combined still often fall short of being an accurate representation of the total picture. As a result, we frequently find that what we had initially believed was not at all the way things actually were. Sometimes we even find ourselves having a change of heart. It is this confrontation that brings us to the crossroads of moving from perception to truth.

Truth on the other hand is a constant that stands unaltered and independent of any and all external factors, opinions, perceptions and analyses. Truth is truth whether or not it is perceived and truth is truth regardless of whether one chooses to reject it or accept it. Water is wet, computers can't think and the earth is spherical regardless of your opinion or perception. Even if you go to your grave believing otherwise about any of the aforementioned, it won't change the truth! Likewise, many of the conclusions about Affirmative Action may very well be based upon erroneous perceptions and therefore would not mirror truth. Yet there are others that may indeed have a sound foundation and thereby bear a degree of merit worthy of serious consideration. Either way you look at it, the task at hand is a rather momentous one, and one that hopefully will be measured up to adequately.

Chapter 3

Finding Common Ground

Can two walk together, except they be agreed? ~ Amos 3:3

Can you make it brother up this long and narrow road? Or do you need somebody to help you carry the load? Well, sit down and let us talk for a little while and then I'll help you walk, I'll help you walk the next mile. Cause we're all just pilgrims and we're traveling the same road. And I want to help you yeah, if I can.

While the lyrics may not be as concise as the words preached by the prophet Amos, they do carry a similar sentiment. There must be something in common if we are to embark upon any expedition requiring a concerted effort. From the words of the prophet one might conclude that any journey involving a team, which does not have at its core a strong and binding force, some mutual conviction or powerful commitment, is from it's inception -- doomed, impossible, a mere exercise in futility. Our case is such that the greatest dynamic with the capacity to affect our outcome is the principle previously put forth -- the yearning for truth. Yet in spite of the Affirmative Action dilemma being as controversial as it is, let's see if we might begin our thousand-mile journey with some small but sound stepping-stones to usher us into our walk together. If we can take the first few and somewhat small steps together, this might enable us to move progressively toward greater enlightenment on our subject. Ultimately it is my hope that this will establish a plot of common ground, and thereby the capacity to keep our perspective with a reasonable degree of focus. To this end we shall first of all seek to accurately define affirmative, and second of all, apply the definition(s) to our immediate situation.

Firstly, turning to *Webster's Third New International Dictionary* in our effort to gain a working definition (as we seek to acquire common ground before walking further) we find the following: affirmative: (1) asserting that the fact is so, (2) giving acknowledgement to a statement as being fact, (3) declaratory of what exist (e.g., affirmative proof that he was in fact a danger to public safety) declaring that this is the state of such a matter, and (4) affirming the existence of certain facts or a particular state of things at the time a contract of insurance is made. Please make a mental note of the latter definition, *affirming the existence of certain facts or a particular state of things.* Now there is yet another definition that should by all means be taken into account in our attempt to illuminate the concept at hand, namely (5) assertive or positive, (e.g., an affirmative or assertive approach to the problem). All of the aforementioned should make it relatively easy to agree, that that which is affirmative is positive. Furthermore, to affirm is to acknowledge or give mental assent to. It has also been the practice of the courts to use the term *affirm*, instead of *swear*, in cases where those who are called to give testimony refuse to comply with the traditional swearing in because of religious convictions. In addition, here are some of its other synonyms: assert, confirm, verify, acknowledge, establish, avow, and the list goes on. It is truly unfortunate that this word *Affirmative*, which is at its core such a powerful means of positive expression, has become stereotypically viewed with such negativity and disdain.

Secondly, having perused Webster to gain insight into the

varied meanings of the word *Affirmative* and thereby providing a fundamental understanding of this most divisive term, let's see how we might make relevant application of its many meanings to the current context of which we speak. Let me suggest that Affirmative Action, if understood within the framework of Webster's definitions might be best described as an assertive or positive action intended to address a particular problem, condition or injustice, that has not only been declared to exist but also acknowledged as fact. The particular wrong happens to be racial discrimination. However, we must be aware that there are those who live in denial regarding the issue of racism. These are they who live in an utopian dream world where everything is ideal. *In their minds* there is presently no such thing as racism, prejudice or discrimination. *In their minds* we live in an evolved and high civilization where racism and discrimination are things found only in the history book accounts of mid-twentieth century America and earlier. On the other hand the realist who is in touch with this world must affirm, he must indeed assert, avow and give recognition to the fact that certain things are so and that these conditions (injustices) do truly exist. They are not mere perceptions of the mind but realities in our society and in our world. Moreover, because they are real, they surround us everyday and can readily be identified if we would but open our eyes. Thus, despite the insistent denials of some, there is indeed *affirmative* proof that the problems of racism and discrimination are in fact fibers in the woven fabric of our society, even in this enlightened age of the 21st century.

Therefore, let me suggest that if properly understood, the Affirmative Action policy of our country (from a historical perspective) might be viewed firstly as a spark flung from the flames of the Fair Employment Laws burning with the echoing theme of *"Liberty and justice for all"*. Secondly, it could be interpreted in the least as an implicit acknowledgement that a particular state, both racist and discriminatory (however distasteful that may seem) does exist within our culture. Thirdly, it could and definitely should be viewed as positive and assertive action designed to arrest racial injustices. This is achieved by introducing legislation that has some capacity to curtail (if not eliminate) the unjust, discriminatory and exclusionary practices that target individuals or groups of people based on sex or gender (not sexual orientation), ethnicity or national origin or race.

Chapter 4

The Golden Rule and Reverse Discrimination

ᢒᢙ

Therefore, all things whatever ye would that men should do to you, do ye even so to them; for this is the law and the prophets. ~ Matthew 7:12

ᢒᢙ

I magine a world where the golden rule is the single rule of law permeating the innermost being of every one of its citizens. Can you see it? Every action, contemplation, and even every decision would focus not on me but on my fellowman, and the latent good or adverse effects of my actions on him. A world no longer guided by "What's in it for me?" but rather, "How will this affect my neighbor, my brother, my fellowman?" Talk about an utopian world. The world of the golden rule is a world where the highest of laws is fulfilled; *Thou shalt love thy neighbor as thyself* (Deut.6:6) and *Love worketh no ill to its neighbor; therefore, love is the fulfilling of the law* (Romans 13:10).

It is the notion of the ideal that should lend us the capacity to diagnose not only the condition of our world but also, and more importantly, that of our own heart. It is the contemplation of the ideal that brings one who hungers and thirsts for righteousness to the sobering state of enlightenment regarding the possibilities for improving relations among members of the human race even though we are so riddled with imperfections.

These imperfections have resulted in a world that is tainted by injustice and indifference, and smoldering with the stench of hatred and bigotry -- our world! But shouldn't our ability to conceive the ideal impregnate us with an inspiration that drives us toward defining solutions for some of the many ails of the current age? Shouldn't the notion of doing what is right, along with the capacity to see the bigger picture, make us more tolerant of any possible adverse affects resulting from doing that, which is both morally and ethically right? Shouldn't the notion of the golden rule, doing to others as you are convinced you would want them to do to you, ever remain before us?

Indeed the golden rule carries unrealized potential and a value that no doubt exceeds the capacity of human comprehension. Every member of the human race possesses some basic or fundamental desires and needs, which are simply inherent with the nature of humanity. There is the need to love and to be loved, the need to feel a sense of worth and value, the need to achieve and contribute in a meaningful way to something greater than ourselves, and the need to feel a soothing sense of security. These are all just as common to humanity as the need for food, water and rest. Furthermore, there should be no doubt that much of the anguish we experience due to the negative fallout from interpersonal relations could be avoided if the golden rule was indeed the rule of life. The golden rule embraces love, which is the fulfillment of the law of God, and since love works no ill to its neighbor, every human need is potentially met -- in the golden rule. With this in mind let's turn our attention to a subject that is frequently at the heart of the opposition encountered by the Affirmative Action policies -- reverse discrimination.

In ongoing discussions, ranging from TV and radio talk-shows to political forums, the issue of reverse discrimination consistently leads the charge in the effort to discredit the Affirmative Action policies as a valid means of impeding the practice of racial discrimination. Quite often (but not always) the debates revolve around the job opportunities extended to minorities, which somehow seems to always refer first and foremost to Blacks. Nonetheless, the argument takes the position that because of Affirmative Action a member of a minority group or as the case may be, someone black, is being employed to fill a position that some qualified white person might otherwise be hired to fill. (By all means please read the previous sentence very carefully. Its ideology and implications will be explored in more detail later on.) Thus the terminology *reverse discrimination,* which has for many become synonymous with Affirmative Action, is utilized to suggest that Affirmative Action discriminates against whites in favor of blacks or other minorities. More succinctly however, the phrase "reverse discrimination" describes how white men in America view Affirmative Action. Consider this excerpt from the *Encyclopaedia Britannica*:

Affirmative Action, in the United States, active efforts that take into account race, sex, and national origin for the purpose of remedying and preventing discrimination. Under the landmark Civil Rights Act of 1964 and subsequent executive orders and judicial decisions, the federal government requires certain businesses and educational institutions that receive federal funds to develop affirmative action programs...

Affirmative Action has been criticized as "reverse discrimination" (usually against white males), but the U.S. commission on Civil Rights argued that only if society were operating fairly would measures that take race, sex, and national origin into account be "preferential treatment". (Micropaedia, vol. 1 pg. 127: Fifteenth Edition 1989).

What a turn of events! Taking this into account, let's look more closely at the idea of reverse discrimination while noting that a true reversal would involve a change of one hundred and eighty degrees. In other words, those who are (1) treated unfairly due to prejudice, (2) discriminated against solely because of skin color or ethnicity, or (3) suffered the loss of numerous employment opportunities due to exclusionary practices, would actually have to swap places with those who claim reverse discrimination. Certainly no reasonably intelligent person with a decent moral foundation would sincerely suggest that the Affirmative Action policies have put white males in a position that reflects the historical plight of African Americans or other minorities. There is truly no comparison and certainly no factual basis for the actual idea expressed by the terminology *reverse discrimination*.

On the other hand, I believe the main intent of those who claim *reverse discrimination* is to propose that Affirmative Action actually perpetuates the very injustice it seeks to resolve. This is usually related in some way to the unpopular notion that corporations must hire a certain number or a specific percentage of employees from among minority groups (which we shall consider further momentarily). This notion is then coupled with the mindset that a select number of employment decisions are made with consideration to race without regard to qualifications in order to meet the demands of Affirmative Action policies. Ultimately, it is the idea of hiring someone of color, non-white if you will, instead of a white person (who would have traditionally gotten the job) that presents the real problem. When this outcome is coupled with the perceptions that precede it, brother you really have a problem! So then, once again we see that an enormous element in this equation is how to affect the perceptions that people possess in order to bring them, if not completely, at least more in line with the truth.

Please keep in mind however, that in reality, and as noted in the *Encyclopaedia Britannica* excerpt, American society has not operated in a manner that is reflective of true justice or fundamental fairness for all people, in spite of the heralding theme of *Liberty and Justice for All*. The very reason for the laws currently on the books is due to the fact that so many people have been violated. Furthermore, if the nature of the violation is racial or ethnic or based upon the color of one's skin, it is only common sense that any legislation proposed to combat such a violation must assume a structure that reflects the nature of the violation. Now let's talk about this issue of perception.

Chapter 5

An Accurate Perspective

And Elisha prayed, and said, Lord, I pray thee,
open his eyes that he may see. - 2 Kings 6:17

In chapter six of 2 Kings, the prophet Elisha and his servant were surrounded by the Syrian army. Syria had been at war with Israel and consequently was engaged in strategizing to achieve victory. However, God was also involved. Working somewhat behind the scene He consistently revealed to Elisha what the Syrian king was planning. Elisha in turn would send word to the king of Israel informing him of things he should be sure not to do and places he should be careful to avoid. The king of Syria became convinced that there was someone in his camp who was a traitor. When he called his officers together and demanded whom the traitor was, one of his servants told him about the prophet Elisha. At hearing this, the king decided to go after Elisha and eventually cornered him. When Elisha's servant had awakened early one morning and discovered that the Syrian army had surrounded them he was panic-stricken. He and Elisha were in a jam and there was clearly no way out of it. So this servant did what almost anyone in his position would do - - he panicked. If we had been there we probably would have heard him say something like, "Look at this mess speaking for

God has gotten us into! What are we going to do now?" Clearly they were outnumbered and the Syrians no doubt had secured all of the possible escape routes. Nonetheless, Elisha's serene disposition was unshaken as he said to his servant, *Fear not; for they who are with us are more than they who are with them* (2 Kings 6:16). Now the biblical account says that the king of Syria had sent horses and chariots and a great host. Yet Elisha claimed, *".... they who are with us are more than they that are with them."* At this point, even if the servant didn't say it, he had to be thinking, "What in the hell are you talking about! Can't you count?" The conclusions that were drawn by this young apprentice of Elisha were the result of a handicapped perspective. He was anxious and flustered due to his inability to perceive anything that was outside the realm of his natural senses. He didn't see the situation from the same vantage point as that of Elisha, and Elisha knew it.

And Elisha prayed, and said, Lord, I pray thee, open his eyes, that he may see. And the Lord opened the eyes of the young man, and he saw; and behold, the mountain was full of horses and chariots of fire round about Elisha (2 Kings 6:17).

Then there is the story of the little girl who was curious about her grandmother's age. She routinely pestered her grandmother, "Come on maw-maw, I want to know how old you are." Of course grandmother always refused. Then one day the little girl went to the kitchen to get a snack and found her grandmother's driver's license on the table. She quickly reviewed the information on the card noting the date of birth. Later that day she approached her grandmother looking like the cat that just swallowed the canary. "Maw- maw, I found out how old you are and I also know that you got an F in sex."

Taking these two illustrations into consideration, we find the common thread of a faulty, if not erroneous, viewpoint. While our perceptions are always powerful, affecting what we hold as truth, they can at times prove potentially hazardous when inaccurate. That is to say, when what we perceive as truth is not consistent with what is truth, we can find ourselves in a serious danger zone. This is especially the case when influencing what we believe about other people or races. So it is, that many view Affirmative Action in a manner similar to the little girl's interpreting the F on her grandmother's license as a failing grade in sex. Then too, others can be compared to Elisha's servant, who was hampered by the limitations of his physical senses. With this before us, let's address some of the opposing viewpoints expressed about Affirmative Action while we also pray, *Lord open our eyes that we may see.*

One of the common thoughts regarding Affirmative Action seems to go something like this: If minorities are now to receive jobs or opportunities which before were unavailable to them due to lack of training, technical skills and formal education, and if as a result of their employment whites who are qualified for positions in these specific areas are being turned away in order to meet government imposed quotas, then the Affirmative Action policy reverses discrimination and thereby perpetuates the injustice which it seeks to remedy. The first notable problem with this trend of thought is the flawed conclusion that Affirmative Action policies advocate employing unqualified persons. Nothing has ever been further from the truth. As a matter of fact, that type of thinking if stretched to the ultimate, might bring you to the ludicrous conclusion that there were either no African Americans in the entire country qualified for professional/executive positions, or that those who were qualified did not apply. Take into account for instance, during the formative stages of the Civil Rights era President Franklin Roosevelt signed *Executive Order 8802.*

Executive Order 8802
WHEREAS it is the policy of the United States to encourage full participation in the national defense program by all citizens of the United States,

regardless of race, creed, color, or national origin, in the firm belief that the democratic way of life within the Nation can be defended successfully only with the help and support of all groups within its borders; and WHEREAS it is the policy of the United States to encourage full participation in the national defense program by all citizens of the United States, regardless of race, creed, color, or national origin, in the firm belief that the democratic way of life within the Nation can be defended successfully only with the help and support of all groups within its borders; and NOW, THEREFORE, by virtue of the authority vested in me by the Constitution and the statutes, and as a prerequisite to the successful conduct of our national defense production effort, I do hereby reaffirm the policy of the United States that there shall be no discrimination in the employment of workers in defense industries or government because of race, creed, color, or national origin, and I do hereby declare that it is the duty of employers and of labor organizations, in furtherance of said policy and of this order, to provide for the full and equitable participation of all workers in defense industries, without discrimination because of race, creed, color, or national origin;

And it is hereby ordered as follows:

1. All departments and agencies of the Government of the United States concerned with vocational and training programs for defense production shall take special measures appropriate to assure that such programs are administered without discrimination because of race, creed, color, or national origin.

2. All contracting agencies of the Government of the United States shall include in all defense contracts hereafter negotiated by them a provision obligating

the contractor not to discriminate against any worker because of race, creed, color, or national origin.

3. There is established in the Office of Production Management a Committee on Fair Employment Practice, which shall consist of a chairman and four other members to be appointed by the President. The Chairman and members of the Committee shall serve as such without compensation but shall be entitled to actual and necessary transportation, subsistence and other expenses incidental to performance of their duties. The Committee shall receive and investigate complaints of discrimination in violation of the provisions of this order and shall take appropriate steps to redress grievances which it finds to be valid. The Committee shall also recommend to the several departments and agencies of the Government of the United States and to the President all measures, which may be deemed by it necessary or proper to effectuate the provisions of this order.

Franklin D. Roosevelt

The White House,

June 25, 1941

Source: US Equal Employment Opportunity Commission

Ref Date: May 17, 2003

<http://www.eeoc.gov/abouteeoc/35th/thelaw/eo-8802.html>

This executive order was issued in 1941, six days before the scheduled march on Washington D.C. which was organized by Asa Phillip Randolph. (Hopefully, you noticed the references to race and ethnic origin along with the term reaffirm.) Randolph intended the march on the capital as a protest against the discriminatory hiring practices of companies doing business with the federal government. When the order states, "provide for the full and equitable participation of all workers", it does not mean equitable participation for whites. The order was not put forth because whites were protesting unfair employment practices. Nor was the order the result of racial profiling that refused to extend to whites the privilege of applying for certain categories of employment opportunities. Neither was it put forth because whites were not being paid fairly. Make no mistake about it, the laws and presidential orders we are talking about were set forth to enhance the potential for non-whites who were also American citizens to be treated with fundamental fairness, human dignity and decency. Should anything less be expected by citizens of the greatest country in the world? However, although President Roosevelt was able to avoid the protest march by signing the order, the march eventually took place twenty-two years later and is memorialized in the 1963 *I Have a Dream* speech delivered by Dr. Martin Luther King Jr. Executive Order 8802 required vocational training to be given without regard to a person's skin color. It also declared that all future defense contracts should include non-discrimination clauses. In addition, the order established a Fair Employment Practice Committee to see that the first two ideas were carried out.

Therefore, to suggest that minorities in general, and African Americans in particular, were not qualified as skilled professionals, might at best be categorized as nothing less than willful ignorance. However, regardless of the qualifications, the predominant order of the day was still *whites only*. Furthermore, the latter order in no way suggests that there were no qualified job candidates among minorities prior to its issuance. What it does convey however is that: (1) the vocational training available to whites who were seeking government contracted work should also be available to people of color who were also interested in those jobs and (2) the government would not continue to supply contracts to corporations that were unwilling to give due consideration to hiring qualified applicants simply because they were not white. Nonetheless, and although unfortunate, the prevalent and inaccurate point of view which suggests that Affirmative Action advocates hiring minorities without regard to qualifications is held by a large number of Affirmative Action opponents.

Chapter 6

Unqualified Minority Employees

A man's gift maketh room for him... - Proverbs 18:16

As I am writing this, it was just last week that I attended an art convention and had the pleasure of meeting Walter and Gwen who both shared from their experiences on issues related to Affirmative Action. Walter, who is now in law enforcement, recalled an experience of a large company in his community during the early 1970's that hired and kept minorities on the employment roster for a period of ninety days. As Walter put it, "Just long enough to ensure the continuance of federal funding." This practice, he says, continued until it was brought into check by the subsequent involvement of the Urban League. Gwen's story on the other hand was a reflection of the candor that often accompanied the bigotry that was quite commonplace during the sixties. She recalled the occasion of being told in no uncertain terms that she was hired only to fulfill the Affirmative Action requirements. After being hired however, she was not given any consideration that would suggest an interest or intent on the part of the employer to get her acquainted with the responsibilities of the position. Furthermore, she was even instructed not to interact with the other employees (who were white). This directive more specifically was purposed to impede her gaining information that would facilitate the development of proficiency in the department. She went on to say that she was being paid and yet not working (fulfilling or performing the duties of the position she held). This is the type of scenario that is often utilized to reflect negatively on the Affirmative Action policies as well as upon the work ethic of black people. However, if the truth be told, it would (in more cases than not) be revealed that the stage is set and the deck stacked so that the picture that is painted is one, which reflects what whites generally desire to convey about that which they do not approve or simply wish to distort. Thus the Affirmative Action policy only made it possible for Gwen to get the position. Her success on the other hand, was directly related to the fact that someone white, in a position of authority and who also possessed a strong moral conscience, became aware of what was going on and put a stop to it. As a result, Gwen began to be handled with common decency and respect. Furthermore, she also began to receive the direction, guidance and assistance, regarding her responsibilities that would normally be given to a new employee. Make no mistake about it, it was the intervention of someone with a sense of fairness and a heart for justice that enabled her to: (1) become proficient in her area of responsibility, (2) contribute to the overall good of the corporation and (3) build the skills and value that would further her career and benefit other corporations years later.

I am also reminded of a Sunday morning, when I was listening to the radio while taking a routine ride to church. As I listened, I learned of a seminary student with an outstanding academic record. He had recently graduated and was actively seeking interviews with churches that were in search of a pastor. This process involved his sending the prospective church a profile of himself indicating how well he had done with his ministerial studies, reflecting on his ideals of pastoral ministry and also including an overview of his strengths. Numerous churches were interested in him and as a result called on him to meet with their governing board and in some cases extended an invitation to give what is called a trial sermon. However, having also received a considerable number of profiles of the churches that were interested in him, he finally came upon one that he believed would be just the right fit. It seemed an ideal match for his personality and his ministerial strengths as well as his priorities. At last the day of his interview came. Needless to say, the church was excited with the prospect of having the young man as their pastor. Unfortunately, all the excitement and the interest came to a screeching halt on the day this young Hispanic met with the prospective new congregation. You see, the congregation was predominantly Caucasian. Upon this new revelation, the qualifications of this young man had no bearing whatsoever. At best, his qualifications merely paled in view of the fact that his ethnicity was not the same as that of the church members. In other words, neither his credentials nor his personality, his love for God nor commitment to ministry, nor any other character strengths or desirable qualities mattered as much as did the fact that he was Hispanic. Even though this account is not one from the secular business world it does convey very well the type of atmosphere, the attitudes and practices that are targeted by the Civil Rights laws, the Fair Labor laws and Affirmative (positive) Action policies.

Yet in the midst of the ongoing debates that often suggests Affirmative Action advocates hiring unqualified individuals from among minority groups, it is seldom reported that in the early to mid sixties the typical white male with a high school diploma earned an average salary that exceeded the earnings of the average black male with a college education. Furthermore, factoring in the widespread *whites only* hiring practices of the day, if ever a case could be made for hiring unqualified or less qualified individuals, the evidence would seem to indicate such a practice in favor of whites and not against them. The Fair Employment Laws however, which embrace Affirmative (positive) Action ideology, sought to address the plight of all minorities. These laws were a direct attack on the systematic exclusionary and discriminatory practices of corporate America and also served as the forerunner to the assault on the disparity in wage compensation due to gender and race. It has been, and still is well documented that women traditionally do not earn salaries comparable to that of men, although performing essentially the same work. Likewise, black men are usually compensated at lower rates than those paid to white males.

In August 2001, France's INSEE statistical institute published a study on wage disparities between men and women. The unexpected finding that the wage gap has widened to women's disadvantage over the past 20 years demonstrates the extent to which the position of women in the labour market and in employment is very different from that of their male counterparts. Men and women of strictly equivalent training and employment do not receive equal pay. The past few decades have seen major advances in `equality´ between men and women in the area of employment. Indeed, the large-scale arrival of women on the labour market, the creation of mainly female-dominated jobs, especially in the public and service sectors, the alignment of the employment behaviour of both sexes (fewer women are interrupting their careers when they have children), and the increased quality of both qualifications among young women and available employment opportunities have altered the role of men and women both economically and socially. However, some indicators, particularly wage-related ones, show that forms of sexual discrimination continue to exist.

Ref Date: May 17, 2003

<http://www.eiro.eurofound.ie/2001/09/feature/ FR0109106F.htm/> http://www.eeoc.gov/35th/thelaw/ epa.html

Black workers (28.8 percent) were more likely than

white workers (21.9 percent) to earn a poverty wage of $8.63 an hour or less. Yet poverty wages among both black and white workers have risen since 1979 levels.

African-Americans with a four-year degree earned a median wage of $16 an hour in 2001, or $4 less than their white counterparts. Yet among the least educated, race is less of a factor for earning potential. Black high school dropouts earned $8.32 an hour versus $8.30 an hour for white high school dropouts.
Ref Date: May 17, 2003
<http://www.policiymatters.org/media/ce.Paycheck.htm/>

Lastly, we will close this segment with the following notation along with its corresponding graphs depicting the disparity in earnings based upon race, gender and education.

The top 1 percent of nonwhite males who had income in 1966 received at least $12,000 (see Fig. 5). However, the top 10 percent of white males received at least $12,000, and the top 1 percent of white males received at least $26,000.

Table 1
Earnings for Males who had Earnings, 1967, By Occupation Group of Longest Job [a]

OccupationGroup	Medians			Means			Proportions [b]	
	W	NW	NW/W	W	NW	NW/W	W	NW
Professional, technical and kindred	$9090	5971	.657	9667	6197	.641	.135	.073
Farmers and farm managers	2804	970	.346	4053	2155	.532	.041	.019
Managers, officials and proprietors	8897	5831	.655	10144	6846	.675	.136	.037
Clerical and kindred	6088	5104	.838	5722	4803	.839	.072	.069
Sales workers	6103	4665	.764	6404	4714	.736	.063	.019
Craftsmen, foremen and kindred	7089	5019	.708	6929	4907	.708	.198	.121
Operatives and kindred workers	5677	4423	.779	5443	4440	.816	.192	.243
Service workers, except private household	3886	3148	.810	4160	3244	.780	.066	.150
Farm laborers and foremen	885	681	.769	1639	1085	.662	.026	.073
Laborers, except farm and mine	2472	2915	1.179	3192	3071	.962	.070	.193
Total	$6290	3780	.601	6621	4009	.605	1.000	1.000
Total for year-round full-time	7396	4964	.671	8131	5125	.630		

Table 3
Males 25 and Over, 1967, By Years of Schooling

Years of Schooling	Medians				Means				Proportions	
	W	NW	NW/W	Marginal Change in Ratio	W	NW	NW/W	Marginal Change in Ratio	W	NW
Elementary	$3936	2889	.734		4533	3269	.721		.283	.473
High School	7047	5015	.712	-.022	7352	5047	.686	-.035	.470	.410
College	9463	7110	.751	.039	10792	7271	.674	-.012	.247	.117
Less than 8	3118	2570	.824		3758	3073	.818		.139	.372
8	4881	3711	.760	-.064	5278	3992	.756	-.062	.144	.101
9 to 11	6408	4545	.709	-.051	6558	4627	.706	-.050	.166	.203
12	7378	5427	.736	.027	7787	5461	.701	-.005	.303	.207
13 to 15	8299	6418	.773	.037	8994	6267	.697	-.004	.104	.057
16 or more	10740	7868	.733	-.040	12089	8223	.680	-.017	.144	.060
Total	$6732	4064	.604		7404	4467	.603			

Ref. Date October 4, 2004
http://www.rand.org/publications/classics/wohlstetter/
R578/R578.chap2.html

Therefore, it should be apparent that the positive measures set forth by the executive orders have had a powerful impact in bringing about legislation designed to achieve equality in pay in addition to facilitating equal employment opportunities for minorities. It should furthermore be quite evident, that the idea that Affirmative Action opens the door for blacks and other minorities to acquire employment in areas where they aren't qualified is totally erroneous. The absence of minorities in non-menial positions was not a matter of qualification but policy. It was an era where the standard of acceptance was, "if you ain't white you ain't right!"

Chapter 7

Now What About Those Quotas?

Wisdom is the principal thing; therefore get wisdom: and with all thy getting get understanding. - Proverbs 4:7

As we approach the issue of quotas let me first restate that the Affirmative Action policies (in a nutshell) are essentially part of a declaration acknowledging that the injustices in American society regarding racial discrimination and employment opportunities, must be arrested if this country is to live up to the creed of liberty and justice for all. How you see things of course, will depend to a large degree on your yearning for truth coupled with how you view the issue thus far. However, I can assure you that public opinion and perception are more the driving forces behind most of the conclusions formulated about the quotas issue than fact. In addition, while one may not necessarily agree with the notion of requiring corporations to maintain numeric data that reflects its hiring practices (as it relates to minorities), the inclusion of minorities has nonetheless been an important factor in facilitating the progress of race relations in American society. There should be little doubt, if any at all, that the inclusion of minorities has brought about increased interaction between races. This interaction helped to foster an environment that was conducive to bringing many independent thinkers to the realization that the color of one's skin is not at all the tell tale factor regarding human worth, intelligence, moral decency, etc. as they were taught to believe in their early years. Furthermore, while some still bark at the idea of so called quotas, there have been too many occasions where laws have been passed that were nothing more than semantic reiterations of laws that were already on the books. For example, everyone talks about the Civil Rights Act of 1964, but very little is ever said regarding the fact that the right to vote was protected by the 15th Amendment of the Constitution which was passed in 1870. Then there are the numerous references to the U.S. Supreme Court decision in Brown vs. the Board of Education (Topeka Kansas, 1954), and the fight against Jim Crow practices, whereas hardly a reference is made to the Civil Rights Act of 1875 that gave blacks the right to equal treatment in public places and transport. Hence, if it were your potential career or your ability to earn a decent income to support a family that was on the line, the so called quotas stipulation would no doubt hold far more appeal than the mere passage of additional legislative verbiage. The following reference regarding the Affirmative Action's quota requirement should prove quite enlightening in an age of misinformation and distortion:

To define Affirmative Action (AA), it is most helpful to explain what AA isn't. The common misconception is that Affirmative Action is a program that requires companies to hire "quotas" of females and minority employees. Affirmative Action is not and never has been quotas. AA is a defined business program that requires qualified employers to maintain records, produce reports and generate statistical analyses identifying their workforce by race and gender. The AA plan identifies any shortfalls (or underutilization) of employees in protected classifications. The program requires employers to make "good faith" efforts to reach out to individuals in these classifications, and provide documentation that members of the protected classes have been given equal opportunities for employment or advancement.

Provided the employer can prove its good faith efforts to "reach out" in accordance with the regulations, they are considered to be in compliance with the program, regardless of any statistical imbalance or underutilization in a protected group.

Separate plans must be developed for persons of color and females and covered veterans and persons with a disability.
Ref Date: July 15, 2003
<http://www.tonsojobs.com>

How about that! You mean Affirmative Action includes women, veterans and those with disabilities? Are you also telling me that Affirmative Action does not and has never required companies to meet quotas? Well welcome to the real world! Instead of debating about quotas that were never imposed, the question that should be asked is, "Why do additional laws have to be passed to ensure the rights of a select segment of the citizenry while the Constitution and Bill of Rights are deemed sufficient to provide those same rights to others of the citizenry without the passage of additional legislation?" Nonetheless, I know there are some who would still contest that circumstances are different now and things have progressed to the extent that we no longer need to adhere to or perpetuate Affirmative Action policies. However, although things have definitely changed, the perception of how different they are is actually to a larger degree a matter of personal experience. That is to say, while it may be true that discriminatory practices today are not at all comparable to what took place thirty or forty years ago, that is only as relevant as the extent to which any given individual no longer experiences setbacks and stagnation in his or her own life. It's in some ways similar to talking about how great the economy is to someone who still can't find gainful employment or whose particular field or industry happens to be suffering amidst an otherwise thriving economy. So then, while I for one will gladly concede that things are not what they were some years ago, I ask you to indulge me for a moment and consider the following.

Within months after I had completed studies in Computer Information Systems, the school's career services office contacted me with some information about a company that was believed to be a viable prospective employer. I was told to expect to hear from them because Career Services had forwarded a copy of my resume' to them. Well sure enough, I was contacted (got the message by way of email) and efforts were made to set up an interview. Unfortunately, the person that I needed to speak with never seemed to be in the office when I called and I conversely was rarely home before late. So we played telephone tag for a while until I decided to go to the woman's office with a copy of my resume' in an effort to get the ball rolling. Unbelievably, she wasn't in but I was able to speak with her co-worker and also left my resume' with him. The following week I contacted her early Monday morning. She apologized, and indicated that she had been out of town but that she would talk with the office staff to determine what day would be good for an interview and then email me with the information. Later that day I received an email which said that while she was out, someone was hired for the position and she had not been told until after talking with me. At the risk of seeming paranoid, my gut reaction was, "Something fishy is going on here!" Well who was at fault, or how can you claim discrimination or prejudice in a situation like the one just described you ask? Yes, I agree that while the circumstances as presented might be suspicious to me; the issue of race discrimination is questionable. One would truly be hard pressed to make a strong and objective case for discrimination or racism based merely on what I have presented. However, this is the point at which it becomes virtually impossible for those who have historically been on the other side of racial discrimination to empathize with, fully understand, conceive, perceive or deduce, the anguish, disgust, frustration, disappointment, and also the swelling anger that is experienced and above all else --the keen sense of intuition developed by a people who have annals of experience dealing with those who are baptized in bigotry and racial hatred or prejudice. But to make the point, one day later, a friend of mine came in asking me about the company and whether I had in fact interviewed with them. He proceeded to tell me that he had been contacted by --get this; the same woman that initially contacted me, and who also informed me that someone else had already been hired without her knowledge. While I am willing to concede that it is possible she might not have known whether someone had been hired, it is also highly unlikely given the size of the company, and the fact that she was from every indication a key player in the hiring process. He then went on to tell me that he was scheduled to interview on Wednesday, for the same position that had allegedly been filled the previous week. My friend by the way is white. With this context in place let's take a look further into the issue of Affirmative Action and quotas.

❧

Executive Order 11246:

On September 24, 1965 President Lyndon B. Johnson signed Executive Order 11246 declaring that contractors doing business with the federal government must satisfy a number of criteria, three of which are listed below:

(1) The contractor will not discriminate against any employee or applicant for employment because of race, creed, color, or national origin. The contractor will take affirmative action to ensure that applicants are employed, and that employees are treated during

employment, without regard to their race, creed, color, or national origin. Such action shall include, but not be limited to the following: employment, upgrading, demotion, or transfer; recruitment or recruitment advertising; layoff or termination; rates of pay or other forms of compensation; and selection for training, including apprenticeship. The contractor agrees to post in conspicuous places, available to employees and applicants for employment, notices to be provided by the contracting officer setting forth the provisions of this nondiscrimination clause.

(2) The contractor will, in all solicitations or advertisements for employees placed by or on behalf of the contractor, state that all qualified applicants will receive consideration for employment without regard to race, creed, color, or national origin.

(5) The contractor will furnish all information and reports required by Executive Order 11246 of September 24, 1965, and by the rules, regulations, and orders of the Secretary of Labor, or pursuant thereto, and will permit access to his books, records, and accounts by the contracting agency and the Secretary of Labor for purposes of investigation to ascertain compliance with such rules, regulations, and orders.
Ref Date: May 17, 2003
Source: US Equal Employment Opportunity Commission
<http://www.eeoc.gov/abouteeoc/35th/thelaw/eo-11246.html>

The order stipulates that companies doing business with those companies receiving federal contracts (money) are also obligated to satisfy the Affirmative Action criteria set forth by the order. It is approached just as if the contracted corporation had a down-line (a term quite familiar to many in multi-level marketing sales organizations).

What is truly astounding is that the order says nothing about hiring a specific number, or a certain percentage of employees from among minority groups. Neither is there present in the language of the order, any terminology that could possibly be misconstrued and thereby lead to the idea that Affirmative Action requires companies to set minority hiring quotas. Even if it did require hiring a certain number of employees from among minority groups, why is that such a bad thing? Here's my theory. Somewhere along the way someone inadvertently (or maybe purposely) concluded that because statistical data was being kept, specific numbers of minorities had to be hired. A subsequent supposition was then added to the quota notion suggesting that any and everything had to be done in order to ensure meeting the numeric requirement. Tagged on to that was an even more inflammatory notion that Affirmative Action by virtue of its alleged mandate to meet hiring quotas not only supported but also advocated hiring unqualified individuals. The inevitable conclusion to this scenario is that people of color must be hired to fill a certain number of positions even when there are no *qualified* minority applicants thereby taking legitimate employment opportunities away from *qualified* whites. Therein lies the essence of the problem. This trend of thinking, to say the least, erroneously paints Affirmative Action as setting forth race as the primary consideration for the employment of people of color. However, the facts indicate that Affirmative Action policies do not advocate, support or facilitate hiring unqualified employment applicants from among minority groups for the express purpose of meeting quotas or otherwise. If it did, one would be hard pressed to justify the terminology "Affirmative Action" as representing something positive. Furthermore, due to the propagation of ignorance, Affirmative Action, even with its potential to bring about much good in our society, continues to face angry and bitter opposition by those who have been duped. Then again, maybe they're not duped! Perhaps it's just the age-old hatred rooted in ignorance and tradition and sustained by an unregenerate heart that is tied to some religion but without a relationship with the true and living God.

Nevertheless, what the executive order actually does is require that corporations maintain documentation reflecting on their hiring practices and processes. This documentation is used to produce reports and to generate statistical analyses identifying their workforce by race and gender. All of the statistical data is used to determine whether the company is in compliance with the rules and guidelines of the order and whether there is any indication that *qualified people of color* are not being extended honest and fair consideration for employment.

Furthermore, each company is also required to develop an Affirmative Action Plan. None of these things, in concert or independently, requires hiring a specific number or percentage of persons from any minority group. The plea, or mandate as the case is here, is that corporate America (dominated by whites) would (1) cease the practice of refusing to give Americans of color the honest and legitimate opportunity to apply for whatever positions or pursue any career they desired and (2) cease the practice of consistently refusing to hire qualified applicants who were American citizens of color, in preference for white applicants (preferential treatment) whom whether equally qualified, more qualified or less qualified, would be hired nonetheless because -- they were white.

Thus Executive Order 11246 had an enormous impact on the momentum of the Civil Rights movement in general. One might even go so far as to say that it was in fact what actually gave the Civil Rights Act of 1964 its teeth. As a result of this executive order numerous opportunities opened to minorities that were heretofore unavailable, being of course reserved typically for white males. African Americans little by little, began to experience increased participation in the life of mainstream corporate America. All businesses, private and otherwise, desiring to keep government contracts had to refrain from expressing the traditionally accepted and expected "whites only" hiring policy. This resulted in the constant and steady, although slow migration, of African Americans into key positions among some of the largest and most notable corporations in the nation. Clearly the Civil Rights Act of 1964 gained considerable momentum due to a corporation's potential loss of government contracts. To qualify for federal funds or contracts, businesses had to divorce the culturally prevalent and despicable "whites only" policy and open their doors to employ qualified American citizens of color. It was the government's way of distancing itself from the ongoing practice of racism in the business world.

So then, when looking at the issue of quotas in the light of the historical backdrop one might very well ask, "What's the problem?" From all appearance the alternative solutions (versus that of setting quotas) within the context of a racist society actively discriminating and excluding targeted groups of people would be: (1) Reverse the discrimination (of course an unacceptable option), which would provide relief for some but in no way attacks the unjust and immoral discriminatory racist practices that have plagued our society for so long, (2) Develop new and revise old legislation to address the prevalent racist and discriminatory practices of the day -- which does no good unless there is a method and a commitment to enforce the legislation (3) Execute option 2 and then leave those in corporate authority on their "honor" to affect the necessary measures to bring about change -- but they had already shown what they would do if left on their own "honor" or (4) Execute option 2 stipulating standards of acceptance regarding the inclusion of those heretofore excluded. While I am sure that there are other possible solutions to this dilemma in the mind of some brilliant genius, none readily come to my feeble mind at the moment. What is most interesting in all of this is that Affirmative Action policies (despite what some would have us believe) managed to come into fruition without actually mandating any quota criteria for hiring minorities.

Therefore, taking the facts into consideration, one would think the majority of Americans would find the Affirmative

Action policies favorable. Furthermore, if anyone has cause to gripe, it would seem those who have been traditionally left out would have more legitimate reasons to dispute and criticize the extent (or limitations) of their newly found inclusion which was long overdue. Certainly, we can all agree that under ideal conditions there would be no need to keep statistics on a corporation's hiring practices or to talk about quotas. That being stated, it also follows that ideally there would not have been cause for the Civil Rights movement, the development of Fair Labor Laws, the issuance of Executive Orders or the mandate of Affirmative Action policies. Moreover, any imposition of so-called quotas would unmistakably set forth the idea that there was no significant degree of confidence (or reason to trust) that the business community as a whole and of its own volition would turn the tide on discriminatory practices. In addition, though never stipulated, quotas as typically referred to merely represent "minimal" inclusion for minorities in areas where they had historically been excluded. The objective of the Affirmative Action policies was to curtail the widespread practice of blatant racism and discrimination throughout corporate America that consistently resulted in the exclusion of qualified American citizens of color from the well-paid professional positions simply because of skin color, ethnicity or gender.

Yet there are those die-hard opponents who are inclined to protest, "I made it without the help of the government and Affirmative Action. Therefore, I believe it is not only unfair but unnecessary!" To this I would ask, "What kind of thinking suggests that unfair, unjust and immoral practices should continue to oppress the masses because of the relatively small number who rise despite the oppression?" It would seem that a society interested in the development of its people to their fullest potential would eliminate, rather than struggle to maintain any condition that serves to impede their development. I am persuaded that careful scrutiny would bring us to the conclusion that far greater good has been attained versus any alleged negative impact resulting from the Affirmative Action policies that have been in effect over the years.

Chapter 8

Historical Summary

Let us hear the conclusion of the whole matter...
~ Ecclesiastes 12:13

To this point we have made an effort to establish clarity by defining the word *affirmative* and noting that it is inextricably tied to the word positive. Moreover, it was also set forth that to "affirm" suggests acknowledgement or mental assent. Specifically, in the case before us, giving mental agreement with regard to the prevalent conditions of injustice related to racial discrimination. Furthermore, we readily observed that there are misconceptions surrounding our subject, and have soundly argued that the misconceptions are indeed a matter of perception and not at all able to be substantiated as a matter of fact. Also, although Affirmative Action facilitates the inclusion of minorities in areas that were historically inaccessible or off limits, its policies have never in truth come close to anything remotely resembling reverse discrimination. In addition, the quota notion has been completely misleading. While the debate over quotas has typically been sustained as a hot topic, it should be noted that the language of the executive order does not even hint at the idea of quotas much less mandate them. Corporations are however required to maintain documented statistical data as a means of tracking their hiring practices and determining compliance with Affirmative Action policy. If there had been a mandated quota criteria it would certainly be a reflection of the moral truth that human nature if left unchecked will gravitate toward that, which is immoral, unjust, and yes -- evil. You might call it the *Lord of the Flies* syndrome. We have also looked at the frequently posited idea that Affirmative Action supports and or advocates hiring unqualified individuals. This of course is closely linked to the erroneous quota belief. It suggests that the imaginary Affirmative Action quota stipulation forces corporations to hire minority employees without regard for employment qualifications. Moreover, we have attempted to impress upon the open-minded reader that any reasonable overview of the historical backdrop would reveal the systematic omission of qualified American citizens of color from the best of opportunities (afforded white males). This omission, in the final analysis, resulted in the denial of true freedom and to a large degree the lack of opportunity to pursue "The American Dream". Without a doubt, an accurate historical perspective and some capacity to empathize with the plight of those who are, or who have been oppressed is no small thing. Certainly one can't be expected to draw intelligent conclusions from a position of literal ignorance. If I may refer to the saying, "Never judge a man until you've walked a mile in his shoes." Experiential knowledge is power indeed.

We live in a world, a culture, and a society where we continue to maintain an enormous degree of civil and moral law? Why not do away with all of these laws and let everyone be guided by ...by what? What has the capacity to make each of us do that, which is right, fair and just? Why not just oblige everyone to honor the golden rule? Yeah, right! We are moral beings, living in a moral universe under the divine and providential direction of a moral God. Consequently, we are now and have always been in need of moral governance. This can be provided either by external means of law or by virtue of moral conscience, which does unfortunately have a capacity for losing its sensibility. If you doubt that's a fact then you are very likely not residing in the inner city and obviously completely unaware of the incessant atrocities reported in the news. The moral law as traditionally accepted in the Christian-Judeo ethic is the objective standard that gives us revelation of the virtues that are consistent with the character and nature of God. These are the laws that have historically been at the very core of the moral and civil laws of the greatest nation in the world. When these are brought to bear upon the heart of an individual by the power of God, it is then that we have the greatest capacity for positive change.

Finally, we can conclude that Affirmative Action is positive action in the midst of an ongoing negative situation. It refers to the actions or measures taken which have both the intent and to some degree the capacity to remedy cyclic patterns of behavior, which are unjust as well as inhumane and subsequently destructive to society as a whole. It should be evident that no society can rise to its greatest potential that does not allow the opportunity for its entire population to rise to theirs. Ultimately, only those who have a heart for God and whose yearning is like that spoken forth by the prophet Amos will be inclined to move toward embracing Affirmative Action and what it truly embodies -- *Let justice run down like waters and righteousness like a mighty stream* (Amos 4:24).

Biblical Insights

The Affirmative Action Dilemma

Chapter 9

The Bible Speaks On Affirmative Action
An Excerpt From the Sermon Series

Let's set the tone. Referring to *Webster's Dictionary* we find the following concerning the word affirmative: (1) asserting that the fact is so, or giving acknowledgement to a statement as being fact (2) declaratory of what exist, e.g., affirmative proof that he was in fact a danger to public safety (3) declaring that this is the state of such a matter, also affirming the existence of certain facts or a particular state of things. I find it significant that it says, "affirming the existence of certain facts or a particluar state of things." However, we must take into consideration the segment of the population who live in denial and still others who live in an utopian society where there is no such thing as racism, prejudice and/or discrimination in this advanced and enlightened age. But to affirm is to say that certain things are so, and that certain conditions do exist. It is the acknowledgement of the realities that are part of everyday life, although not necessarily yours. Lastly for our consideration is the definition of "assertive" or "positive". The example being, *an affirmative approach to the problem.* Or we might say, an assertive or positive approach to the problem. Thus, Affirmative Action is positive or assertive action initiated to address a particular problem that is declared to exist. Though there are those who say there is no problem, the evidence indicates otherwise and Affirmative Action comes into play as a positive measure that is intended to curtail if not eliminate the problem. More specifically, in our case the problem of unjust and discriminatory practices executed against individuals or certain groups of persons because of their race, national origin, gender or skin color.

Incidentally, this morning brother Morrison mentioned an experience he had years ago where he was earning one dollar an hour while a co-worker, who was white and with no more qualifications than he, earned two dollars an hour doing the same job. That is a pretty good description of discrimination, and Affirmative Action is designed as a positive approach to resolving the problem of unjust treatment due to racial or ethnic differences (albeit the current illustration leans more toward regulations regarding Fair Labor Laws). Obviously, race should not play a role in determining the level of compensation a person receives from an employer. Yet anyone who is honest will admit, that for quite some time it didn't matter what level of skill or the type of credentials you possessed, if you were black there was virtually no way you were going to earn a salary or wage comparable to that of someone white. However, most of us would agree that in an ideal world, qualifications coupled with an individual's performance and other valuable assets would be sufficient for determining a fair level of pay. In our immediate context, Affirmative Action has to do with addressing the practices of exclusion, oppression, disfranchisement and dehumanization of any group(s) of people on the basis of race, national origin, gender or skin color. Taking these factors into consideration, what reasonably intelligent and just person would oppose an Affirmative Action policy? A policy designed to provide equal opportunity for all people without regard for external physical factors or traits. Well as we shall see, neither injustice nor Affirmative Action is something unique to American culture, but both however have a long history that spans from ancient times to the present.

Chapter 10

Affirmative Action In Ancient Egypt

And it came to pass in those days, when Moses was grown, that he went out unto his brethren, and looked on their burdens: and he spied an Egyptian smiting a Hebrew, one of his brethren. And he looked this way and that way and when he saw that there was no man he slew the Egyptian and buried him in the sand. ~ Exodus 2:11

This verse introduces us to the Israelites in Egypt, under bondage and oppressed. They were in what is described as bitter bondage. Oppressed, in bondage, and subjugated with the foot of Egyptian might resting heavily upon their necks and no apparent means of deliverance. It is the first chapter of the book of Exodus however that gives us the underlying factors resulting in their subjugation. At the outset things in Egypt were actually favorable due to the role of Joseph, a Hebrew, who was promoted to the position of supreme governor of Egypt and was second in power only to Pharaoh himself. You can read the account of Joseph's life in Genesis chapters 37 thru 50. The Hebrews from all indication continued to do well and remained in the good graces of the Egyptians even after Joseph's death until a new linage of kings or Pharaohs came to power.

Now there arose a new king over Egypt, which knew not Joseph (Exodus 1:8)

This was the turning point for the Hebrews' pleasant stay in Egypt. It is this shift in power among Egyptian Pharaohs that brings us to the all-familiar story of the slaughter of innocent Hebrew male infants. This atrocity was perpetrated during the early stages of what proved to be an extensive and grueling oppression. But have you ever stopped to ponder what might have been the causative factor(s) behind the oppression? What is it that causes one to feel it necessary to oppress another? The Bible not only tells us that the Israelites were under Egyptian domination, it also tells us what brought about the subjugation. No, it does not require a complex or in depth discourse, nor does it require the academic astuteness of a PhD to comprehend. As a matter of fact, it is as simple and elementary as a single four-letter word - - FEAR!

... behold the children of Israel are more and mightier than we: Come on, let us deal wisely with them; lest they multiply, and it come to pass, that, when there falleth out any war, they join also with our enemies, and fight against us....(Exodus 1:9,10).

Yes fear! Pharaoh was afraid of the Israelites' potential power. He was consumed with the thought of what *might happen* if their increasing male population was to unite with the enemies of Egypt to fight against him. His fear, however unjustified it may have been and however unlikely the scenario he envisioned, was nonetheless real in his mind. He was afraid of what he perceived to be the summation of their unified strength utilized in battle against the Egyptians. He was afraid of the degree to which he believed they could achieve and excel. Indeed, he was fearful of the possibility, regardless of how remote it might have been, that Israel would rise up and assume an active role in bringing about the subjugation of Egypt. He was not afraid of reality but of possibility. So it was fear that served as the motivational force, which drove this new Pharaoh to establish an institutionalized oppression of the Hebrew people. It was an oppression that lasted approximately four hundred years, and as a result the Hebrews had forgotten whom they were and whose they were. They were the objects of an oppression that no doubt, seemed like an eternity of dehumanization, rigor, and affliction. After four hundred years, now void of all hope or vision of a meaningful future, they could see no further than the brick pits that engulfed them daily. No longer could they recall their heritage as one having any worthwhile significance. No longer could they envision or identify with the nobility of Joseph, their ancestor. Like black people in America, oppressed too long! Oppressed because someone was afraid.

And it came to pass in those days, when Moses was grown that he went out unto his brethren...(Exodus 2:11)

As we follow the biblical chronology of Moses' life we are able to determine that he is approximately forty years of age at this time (Acts 7:23). Surely the author does not intend to suggest that Moses was not grown until reaching the age of forty. The writer's intent is probably a suggestion with regard to his maturity and his awareness of God's purpose for his life. It is at this point in his life that Moses enters more fully the self-realization that ultimately brings him to the fulfillment of that purpose for which he had been saved (as an infant) from the Pharaoh's edict. Whatever our writer's initial intent, it appears quite apparent that Moses spent a significant portion of his life without any notable public identification with his own race or heritage. He lived his life in the manner of what we might call "passing as an Egyptian" and subsequently was unquestionably the beneficiary of preferential treatment. He lived in an Egyptian society, benefited from the highly developed educational institutions of Egypt, thoroughly assimilated Egyptian culture, spoke the Egyptian language, wore Egyptian clothing, lived in the comfort of Egyptian royalty and above all else was immune to the adverse consequences of being a Hebrew during a time of Hebrew persecution (Acts 7:21–23).

One might say that it was Affirmative Action on a limited scale. No doubt the probability is greater than not that there were many Israeli men who had just as much, if not more ability than that possessed by Moses. The biggest difference however, was that Moses had unlimited access to all that Egypt had to offer while the other Hebrew men were restricted by the oppression imposed by the Egyptian society. Moses therefore, was able to excel, develop his potential and achieve greatness (Acts 7:22). It will forever remain untold how many architects, mathematicians, physicians, astronomers or scientists might have worked their lives away in the brick making business under forced servitude because they were denied the opportunity to do otherwise. But is society to blame when one of its citizens fails to reach their fullest potential? That might be too much to say without assessing each situation within its particular context. On the other hand, it should never hold true that society was instrumental in keeping any person or group of persons segregated from the opportunities that would serve to enhance their development and overall good. Remember, Pharaoh was afraid of the potential unified power of the Hebrew nation (Exodus 1:10). There was no justifiable reason for any Pharaoh to fear one man, and certainly not one that had been reared in his own household. Subsequently, while multitudes of Hebrew boys died because of the Pharaoh's edict (Exodus 1:15-22), Moses' life was spared. After all, he was only one child.

Thus although Moses benefited from all that Egypt had to offer, and possibly to some degree enjoyed the favor of Pharaoh, this was nonetheless God's affirmative (positive) action plan. It was a plan designed to bring an end to the toilsome abuse, the steadfast agony and dehumanization brought about by centuries of enslavement. This was a positive action plan that purposed to bring the people of God from the bondage of Egypt to a land flowing with milk and honey, and it did. Although it may have initially appeared limited in scope, it proved in the end to be all encompassing. God's plans and purposes are more often than not, much greater than we are able to envision. *For eye hath not seen, nor ear heard, neither has entered into the heart of man the things that God hath prepared for them that love Him* (1 Corinthians 2:9).

As a matter of fact, the scope of God's Affirmative Action plan goes considerably beyond the mere deliverance of the Israelites from Egyptian bondage. God's Affirmative Action plan is global in its scope and thereby extends itself to all the people of every nation. This was set forth in God's covenant and promise to Abraham, *...in thee shall all families of the earth be blessed* (Genesis 12:3; Galatians. 3:16). However, what is magnified in the Exodus account is a God of compassion and mercy who sees the brokenness of his people.

And the Lord said, I have surely seen the affliction of my people who are in Egypt, and have heard their cry by reason of their taskmasters; for I know their sorrows; And I am come down to deliver them...(Exodus 3:7,8).

This is testimony of a God who realizes his people are without the wherewithal to do anything that will bring about any meaningful change in their predicament. This is not just a story but *His Story*. The Exodus was not merely a long awaited deliverance from Egypt, but also a type or picture of the ultimate redemption of humanity from the bondage of sin. This is *His Story* of how He enters the realm of human existence, in the midst of our brokenness, in the midst of our affliction, while we are yet tainted and terminally scarred by sin. *For all have sinned and come short of the glory of God* (Romans 3:23). He finds us hopeless, hapless, helpless and in bondage to sin. God finds us not in order to pronounce the final sentence of judgment upon deserving sinners, but conversely to affirm his love. *But*

God commendeth his love toward us, in that, while we were yet sinners, Christ died for us (Romans 5:8). He finds us not to consign us to eternal damnation, but to execute the positive measures that will bring us healing (Luke 4:18), to break the yoke of the oppressor and to set us free from the bonds that have held us captive for so long (John 8:33-36). God comes not to destroy us but to deliver us (Exodus 3:7-9). Whether we would vote for it or not God has implemented it. Whether we accept it or not God still offers it -- Affirmative Action! *For whosoever shall call upon the name of the Lord shall be saved* (Romans 10:13). For a sin-sick race of rebellious beings prone to hate not only one another but God himself, he responds with -- Affirmative Action! *...Father forgive them; for they know not what they do* (Luke 23:34). We all look for positive things to happen in our lives, but positive things cannot happen without Affirmative (positive) Action. The God and Father of our Lord and savior Christ Jesus brought the greatest Affirmative Action plan ever implemented, into fruition some two thousand years ago in the person of Christ Jesus who offered himself sacrificially for the sins of humanity.

> *To wit, that God was in Christ reconciling the world unto himself, not imputing their trespasses unto them, and hath committed unto us the word of reconciliation. Now, then we are ambassadors for Christ, as though God did beseech you by us; we pray you in Christ's stead, be ye reconciled to God. For he hath made him, who knew no sin to be sin for us, that we might be made the righteousness of God in him* (2 Corinthians 5: 19-21)

> *For God so loved the world that he gave his only begotton son that whosoever believeth in him should not perish but have everlasting life. For God sent not his son into the world to condemn the world, but that the world through him might be saved. He that believeth on him is not condemned; but he that believeth not is condemned already, because he hath not believed in the name of the only begotton son of God. And*

this is the condemnation, that light is come into the world and men loved darkness rather than light, because their deeds were evil (John 3:16-19)

Chapter 11

Race Discrimination In the New Testament Church

And in those days when the number of the disciples was multiplied there arose a murmuring of the Grecians against the Hebrews because their widows were neglected in the daily ministration. - Acts 6:1

This verse of scripture introduces us to the church during a period of growth, which was apparently associated with some uncomfortable if not surprising growing pains. There seems to be a peculiar relationship between growth and the difficult challenges that often arise in conjunction to that growth. As the church increased in number, there developed a stream of discord concerning the administration of the benevolent ministry. Though we might not be shocked by the idea of the church experiencing internal difficulties, it is notable that this problem was one with ethnic overtones. Giving careful attention to this passage we see that the Grecian widows were being neglected during the regular distribution of goods. This treatment became a source of discord between the Grecian and native Hebrews. More importantly, it was the foundation upon which Satan would initially disrupt and ultimately attempt to destroy the nature and spirit of the fellowship that previously infused the body of believers - - true *koinonia*. Keep in mind that these widows were not accidentally overlooked but systematically and habitually either omitted or handled in such a manner that they were left feeling that the process for distributing support to widows was partial to those women who were not Hellenists (Greek speaking Jews). Hence, they were not getting a fair portion of the goods distributed. What do you suppose might be the reason for this routine neglect? Could it have been due to their arriving after the designated time for receiving goods? Perhaps it was caused by an insufficient supply of goods in proportion to the number of widows seeking assistance. Well, while it would be preferable that one of these two reasons was the basis for the omission, this unfortunately is not the case. The reality is that we are confronted with what might be considered unthinkable -- there was racial discrimination in the early New Testament (Christian) church! Yes, they were actually being neglected or slighted during the daily distribution of goods, without any consideration for how badly they might have been in need, solely because those who were in charge of this ministry were given to prejudice. More specifically, what we would no doubt refer to today as profiling.

Taking into account everyone in the early church willingly contributed what goods they possessed to the common good of all; the idea of race discrimination seems at best an illusion.

Neither was there any among them that lacked; for as many as were possessors of lands or houses sold them, and brought the prices of the things that were sold, and laid them down at the apostle's feet; and distribution was made unto every man according as he had need. (Acts 4:34-35)

The church was well able to meet the needs of each of its members due to the spirit of generosity that permeated the community. However, somewhere along the way the ministry of benevolence for widows went sour. More concisely, what we find is that when the goods were being distributed, those widows who were of strict Jewish heritage received preferential treatment, or we might euphemistically say that they had *first dibs on the goods*. On the other hand, those widows whose heritage was linked to that of the Greek's (Hellenism) culture were characteristically slighted, profiled, or discriminated against during the benevolent distribution. In addition, we are not informed in any respect as to how long this situation persisted. What we do know however, is that at some point along the course of events the situation erupted, causing notable friction and discord among the fellowship of believers.

Although it is generally agreed that everyone has a breaking point, it is not uncommon to find that those who are being taken advantage of, frequently give the benefit of the doubt to their abusers. Those suffering abuse will often rationalize to convince themselves that what is taking place is something other than what it actually is. Giving all consideration to tolerance, there is still nevertheless a point at which you finally declare, *"That's all I can stand and I can't stands no more."* Should that in any way surprise us? I think not. Is it logical to expect harmony and unity to thrive under the same roof where injustice abides? Should we expect to find love, trust and peace where there is ill will, neglect and abuse? It is a contradiction of reason to continue rubbing sand paper against wood and at the same time expect the wood to retain its rough texture. Consequently, there arose amidst the Christian fellowship contention, discord and friction. How then would this problem be addressed? Where should the afflicted go to voice their grievances? Who would be concerned enough, fair enough, and objective enough to hear them out and sincerely look into the allegations of unfair treatment and habitual neglect? Well the issue was brought right where it should have been brought; to those who were in authority.

Chapter 12

The Elected Officials – Great and Effective Leadership

Then the twelve called the multitude of the disciples unto them, and said, It is not fitting that we should leave the word of God and serve tables. Wherefore, brethren look among you for seven men of honest report, full of the Holy Spirit and wisdom, whom we may appoint over this business. But we will give ourselves continually to prayer, and to the ministry of the word. ~ Acts 6:2-4

Although we are not told exactly how, the twelve apostles nonetheless became aware of the disruption caused by the ongoing discrimination during the distribution to the widows. The context of the passage would indicate that those who presented the grievance expected that the apostles would become directly involved (hands-on) in implementing the resolution to this situation. Is it strange that this first century church somehow arrived at the conclusion and evidently embraced as fundamental, the idea that those who were leaders by virtue of their calling or position should be at the forefront of affecting justice? It appears unquestionable that the apostles were sought out and called upon to ensure that all members of the congregation were treated impartially, fairly, justly and with the dignity befitting each and every member of the human race. What is implicit in this passage is the principle that those in positions of leadership have a moral obligation toward, as well as a degree of responsibility for all of those affected by their realm of authority. *Obey them that have the rule over you, and submit yourselves; for they watch for your souls, as they that must give account* (Hebrews 13:17). Certainly we would desire and even insist, that those who watch for our souls (as well as any others in authority) be objective, levelheaded, honest and wise. The apostles demonstrated their wisdom by delegating the task of resolving the discrimination to a committee and thereby not allowing themselves to be drawn away from their most paramount task, which would have proven detrimental to the ministry. They not only directed that the committee be appointed, but also set forth the qualities that were imperative for each committee member to possess - - honesty, full of the Spirit of God and wisdom.

Webster's Third New International Dictionary defines honest as (1a) free from fraud or deception, (b) unquestioned authenticity, (3a) of a creditable nature: of good reputation: respectable and (4a) characterized by integrity. It appears quite apparent that in the minds of the apostles, the ability to resolve the conflict was commensurate to the character of leadership and the relationship of each leader with the God of all creation. These first century fishermen and unlearned men did not see setting up a new system for distributing the goods as the answer. In our age of enlightenment however, we more frequently than not have proposed changes in systems of government as a means of solving problems. However, the fact of the matter is that whenever people suffer under a system of government it is always because of corrupt, immoral, insensitive, greedy and uncompassionate people and not because the system of government, which can only be wielded by those in power, is bad or evil. Nonetheless, it often seems that popular opinion favors the point of view, which suggests that implementing a more effective system would be the best approach to resolving problems. But how productive is an effective system of operation that is administered by dishonest (corrupt) leadership. Most of us can recall hearing reports of the thousands of dollars misappropriated (stolen) in various non-profit organizations, government agencies designed to help the less fortunate, and let's not forget the large corporations where workers can loose their entire pension because the people in positions of authority and power are dishonest. The odds are likely that you even know someone who does not vote due to their philosophy that all politicians are crooks. Even though there is a considerable amount of corruption in politics, we continue to hear that the solution to our woes is in electing this or that party to this or that office. Thus, while the top seat in Washington D.C. seesaws between political parties, we seem to remain frustrated with the challenges of a new day and still exhausted with our inability to find solutions to the conflicts of yesteryear.

The apostles however, realized that the heart of man was at the core of any justice executed or injustice perpetrated. Therefore, a resolution to the discrimination would be dependant upon the ability to secure leaders who possessed an unwavering foundation as well as an abiding presence of the Spirit of God in their lives. It is when these qualities are evident that leaders are most apt to possess the character, the internal fortitude and the commitment to do what is just and right despite the opposition. Also, in the absence of wisdom, believers have free access to God who promises, that when asked, he will supply whatever is lacking. *If any of you lack wisdom, let him ask of God, who giveth to all men liberally, and upbraideth not, and it shall be given him* (James 1:5). On the other hand, a society that divorces God will find itself with leaders who are famished of these qualities and subsequently a system of law that is progressively diminished in its capacity to administer or uphold justice. Deep down within, we know the benefit and the power of leaders who are honest, full of integrity, wisdom and the spirit of God.

Therefore, in the final analysis the weightier issue of the day on the subject of leaders is not with regard to one's years of experience or the lack thereof, nor as to the educational credentials possessed. The issue of leadership has to do with the spirit and heart. Consider the following passages:

Not by might, nor by power, but by my Spirit, saith the Lord of hosts (Zech. 4:10)

For rulers are not a terror to good works, but to the evil. Wilt thou, then, not be afraid of the power? Do that which is good, and thou shalt have praise of the same; for he is the minister of God to thee for good. But if thou do that which is evil, be afraid; for he beareth not the sword in vain; for he is the minister of God, an avenger to execute wrath upon him that doeth evil (Romans 13:3,4)

And I have filled him with the Spirit of God, in wisdom, and in understanding, and in knowledge, and in all manner of workmanship (Exodus 31:3)

Give, therefore, thy servant an understanding heart to judge thy people, that I may discern between good and bad. For who is able to judge this thy great people (1 Kings 3:9)?

The fear of the Lord is the beginning of knowledge, but fools despise wisdom and instruction (Proverbs 1:7)

For the Lord giveth wisdom; out of his mouth cometh knowledge and understanding (Proverbs 2:6)

Although the apostles stipulated wisdom as criteria for election, it does not necessarily follow that these seven men were endued with any significant amount of earthly knowledge. Solomon is said to have had all wisdom and he didn't have a degree from Harvard or Princeton. As a matter of fact, he didn't even have an Associate Degree. If wisdom would be defined as the ability to use knowledge effectively, it becomes clear that everyone who has a "degree" of knowledge is not necessarily wise - - hence the term "educated fool". Yes, if there were ever a time when we needed leaders with understanding, insight, wisdom and a heart to do right, we need them now. However, if the Bible is true, we should be rushed to the ICU (intensive care unit) because true wisdom and understanding are inextricably tied to the person and nature of God and we as a people/nation seem to be moving further and further away from God. There is more and more concern expressed about what is politically correct while at the same time we see a steady movement away from that which is morally right! Far more effort goes into avoiding offending a person whose belief system varies from that which is traditionally viewed as being consistent with the Christian-Judeo ethic versus any concern about offending the God of the universe. Indeed we live in an age where wisdom and understanding are in short supply. Nonetheless, the qualities that characterized the seven are a necessity for leaders who would successfully confront the complex and sensitive issues of the day.

Subsequently, under the apostles' direction, a committee of seven disciples (honest and full of the Holy Spirit and wisdom), selected not by the apostles but by the people from among the people, was appointed to oversee the regular distribution of goods to the widows. In essence, the apostles were actually responsible for implementing what might be regarded as an Affirmative Action program. The committee's main objective was to resolve the unjust neglect the Grecian widows experienced during the distribution of goods, and thereby bring healing in the midst of an atmosphere that had become negative, divisive and contentious. This committee was charged with getting results and not merely passing new rules or implementing some type of feel-good legislation to address the concerns of the disgruntled. The primary and immediate task of these seven men, elected by the people, was to bring an end to the ongoing systematic exclusion of Grecian widows during the distribution of support for widows.

While these neglected women were privileged to receive whatever supplies would be provided, they were also by virtue of their status equally entitled to those goods, which were designated for the support of the widows within the Christian community. However, as has already been noted, the supplies were indubitably being distributed in an unfair manner and the Grecian widows complained that they were being slighted. If the seven men elected to the committee could achieve their goal, the fellowship would find the contention replaced with contentment, discord displaced by unity and the murmuring drowned with praise. The saints would once more experience the blessing of walking in the mercy and justice of God.

Chapter 13

Lessons On
Unjustified Hatred

*If a man says, I love God, and hateth his brother, he is a
liar... ~* I John 4:20

What is truly amazing to observe in all of this is how human nature tends to focus upon and magnify our differences rather than accentuating our commonalities. How could it be that one group of Jews saw themselves as being more deserving and privileged than another group of Jews. Were not both groups of widows Jews indeed? Did not each and every one of them belong to this fellowship of the household of faith? Were not all of them children of Abraham, joint heirs with Christ, children of God and members of the same heavenly and spiritual family? Even amidst the glory of the early church, which most would hail as the period of her purest spirituality, we see the evidence of human prejudice piercing the eternal Shekinah (she-ky'-nah, the visible representation of the presence and glory of God) and witnessing to the fallen nature of mankind. Yes it is sad, but true, that we seem to give more weight to the differences found in race and in skin color versus the value and worth that can be derived from similarities in integrity, character, faith, principle and conviction. However, when we speak of racial hatred it should be noted that it is mostly a trait learned and cultivated during the formative years of childhood versus something that is inherent in the behavior or personality. Let me take a moment to emphasize this with two illustrations.

I recall an episode of the original sci-fi television show *Star Trek,* in which one extraterrestrial humanoid was in pursuit of another. These two were the last survivors from their world. All of the others perished in a bitter and unending war founded upon an intense and undying hatred for one another. The captain and crew of the starship Enterprise could not understand what either of them saw in the other that was so detestable. Other than the variations in facial features they were the spitting image of one another. There was nothing in their physical appearance that would readily distinguish one from the other. Both of them were split right down the middle, snow white on one side and tar black on the other. Then it happened. While on the bridge of the starship Enterprise, these two engaged in a physical battle resulting in a static discharge with the visual effects of being electrocuted. Once the two finally let go of each other, Loci, the aggressor, stepped back and shouted at the other (whose name was Beal), "You half-white!" The members of the crew who were on the bridge stood stunned as they tried to digest the words that had just been spoken. At this point Captain Kirk diplomatically intervened in an effort to convey that the two were indeed very much alike. He no doubt was communicating what everyone else was thinking at that very moment, "Look at yourself. You're just as white as he is." Insisting that the two of them were virtually identical, he urged Loci to put aside his unjustified hatred in order to preserve their race. Then Loci replied, "Captain are you blind? The difference between us is obvious. Look at us!" Loci stood waiting, as if he expected a response. A deafening silence came over the bridge. As each officer starred at Loci you could hear them thinking - - "The man is insane!" Finally, sensing that no response was likely, Loci blurted out, "Beal is black on the right side, ...all of his people are black on the right side!" Fascinated by what appeared totally illogical Mr. Spock raised his right eyebrow. Then Loci, frustrated with the inability of the crew to grasp the obvious, uttered his concluding words in defense of his hatred, - - "All of my people are white on the right side."

The other example that demonstrates how racial hatred and stereotyping are passed comes from my personal experience. It was during the year that I first began pastoring. I had been assigned to a church that was in a rural area requiring a thirty-minute ride across the lake along with another thirty to forty-five minutes before getting to the church. However, since it was essentially considered a ride to the "country" and having quite a few dirt roads to travel, there wasn't much use for trying to locate the place on a map. The method of finding the church was that of being sure to talk to someone that had previously served as the pastor. Well, needless to say, either the directions were not very good or I didn't follow them correctly and I ended up getting lost. Yeah I know, if you're a woman you are probably saying, "What else is new when a man is at the wheel?" Anyway, I decided that I'd put my male ego aside and pull in somewhere to ask whether they knew of the church and if so how could I get to it. So as I came to the next trailer home on the road I pulled over, got out of the car, and bravely knocked at the door somewhere in the vicinity of nine o'clock on a Sunday morning. After waiting for a short moment, a little boy with blonde hair and bluish gray eyes who was somewhere between the ages of 4 and 6 came to the door. Having opened the door and seeing me standing there he turned around and said, "Daddy it's a nigger."

The Bible says in Proverbs 22:6, *Train up a child in the way he should go and, when he is old, he will not depart from it.* Some have apparently misinterpreted this as "Train up a child in the way *you want* him/her to go." It is unfortunate but quite apparent that much of the racial hatred we find in the world, if not all of it, is inherited. That is to say, it is passed on from one generation to the next. This situation is essentially the same process that creates or sustains the ongoing problem of terrorism in today's world. Young impressionable children are taken advantage of as their hearts and minds are filled with doctrines that establish a basis for hatred and violence. Being children however, they are truly victims and clearly victimized! They are discipled, cultivated, and nurtured just like a farmer raises his crop. Their life's reality is based on faulty perceptions that are virtually impossible for them to shatter. Having been carefully sheltered and indoctrinated they have unknowingly fully surrendered their capacity for individual thought on, as well as assessment of, the hatred that permeates their lives. It is interesting to note in our culture, those who suffer with this hatred seem most often to be fairly uneducated and quite limited in terms of their exposure to communities beyond the one in which they were raised. Furthermore, when put to the challenge of articulating their views they are merely parroting that which has been deeply embedded in their mind since childhood. However, make no mistake about it, the club of racial hatred does have its share of members who possess a considerable amount of formal education. Albeit in my opinion true education does bear some capacity to make a significant positive impact on the general mindset that one develops regarding race.

Let me conclude this segment using the previous *Star Trek* illustration. Loci's hatred of Beal should be clear evidence that racial hatred is mostly inherited. It is passed from generation to generation like a baton in the 400-meter relay of a track meet. If Beal had been fortunate to have known a top-notch plastic surgeon, or if the ship's physician, Dr. McCoy, could have reversed the pattern of his skin pigmentation prior to his meeting Loci, they might have been the best of friends. Loci's hatred was not based upon any specific character trait about Beal that he found detestable. Nor was it due to some transgression on Beal's part against him. Loci had learned to hate by way of those who were responsible for his rearing. Yes, it was through constant exposure to those who were not merely devoted to hating but also committed to the perpetuation of that hatred by planting it in the hearts of their young and innocent children. When Loci looked at Beal he saw only what he had been taught to see and he felt only what had been cultivated in the soil of his heart -- a deep and undying hatred! The hatred that at one time belonged to someone else was now his. God will surely hold accountable all those who participate in manufacturing innocent children into disciples of racial hatred from generation to generation.

And ye fathers, provoke not your children to wrath, but bring them up in the nurture and admonition of the Lord (Ephesians 6:4)

But whosoever shall offend one of these little ones who believe in me, it were better for him that a millstone were hanged about his neck, and that he were drowned in the depth of the sea (Matthew 18:6)

Chapter 14

Seven Distinguished Men

And the saying pleased the whole multitude; and they chose Stephen, a man full of the Holy Spirit, and Philip, and Prochorus, and Nicanor, and Timon, and Parmenas, and Nicolas, a proselyte of Antioch. ~ Acts 6:5

Who were these seven men who were called upon to bring justice to the Grecian widows and restore the harmony of this early Christian body. There is not very much said about them other than the fact that they each met all of the qualifications set forth by the apostles. Of course there is the seventh chapter of Acts that tells us of the martyrdom of Stephen. Also, we find an account of Philip in the eighth chapter witnessing to an Ethiopian eunuch. Other than these two references there is not much that could serve to further our insight on these seven outstanding leaders. However, a more careful look into the meaning of each of their names does prove rather interesting. Examining the origin of each of these names we are able in most cases to find some degree of correlation between its meaning, the likely character of the man and the outcome of the challenge before them. Let's take the names as they are given to us in the list of Acts chapter six verse five.

First is Stephen (ste-fa'-nos) meaning to twine or wreathe a crown such as those awarded in the games or those worn to esteem honor in the highest degree. Stephen, who appears to have been distinguished from the others by notation of an extraordinary anointing in his life, ultimately displays a character and inner fortitude that is exemplary of the crown of life. He without a doubt was indeed highly esteemed among those of this first century fellowship. Second is Philip, the only one of the seven whose name does not readily convey some thought that relates to the task given these men. The name is comprised of two words, the first of which refers to fondness and the second to horses, hence the meaning, fond of horses. Third is Prochorus, (prokh'-or-os) which is composed of the Greek preposition *pro* that often means *fore, prior* or *in front of.* This preposition is followed by *choros,* which has an uncertain derivation. However, it appears to have given rise to our word choir and also seems to convey the idea of celebration. Certainly, there could be no celebration or release of exuberant praise among the people until the justice of God had become evident in their midst. *Strong's Exhaustive Concordance* defines it as a ring or round dance. Thus the literal meaning is before the dance. Fourth is Nicanor (ny-ka'-nor) meaning success or victorious. It also has close relations to the terms conquer and overcome. The scriptures make it clear that the people of God are more than conquerors (Romans 8:37). We are further assured that in all things God has purposed us to be victors and not victims (II Corinthians 2:14). Make no mistake about it, God expects his people to be the head and not the tail. Listen to the words given to Joshua when he took the reigns of leadership.

Only be thou strong and very courageous, that thou mayest observe to do according to all the law, which Moses, my servant, commanded thee; turn not from it to the right hand or to the left, that thou mayest prosper wherever thou goest. This book of the law shall not depart out of thy mouth, but thou shalt meditate therein day and night, that thou mayest

observe to do all that is written therein; for then thou shalt
have good success (Joshua 1: 8,9)

I am persuaded that these men, being full of faith and the Holy Spirit, did not set their eyes on success but on God who was able to bring success. They evidently realized that a reverence for the word coupled with obedience to the word, would be the key to overcoming the discord, triumphing over Satan and conquering the spirit of racial prejudice. Thanks unto God who always causes us to triumph... for we are more than conquerors through him! God has promised victory and has graced his people with a spirit that can overcome any obstacle that might be encountered. He has foreordained that no weapon formed against us will prosper! The apostle Paul could say in essence, I've been knocked down but not knocked out! However, let us never forget that these gifts are always and only accessible to those who are committed to loving and walking with the God of the universe who is also the God of justice. Fifth is Timon, rooted in a word that carries the idea of high esteem, valuable, honor and precious. Certainly men of integrity and character are both precious and invaluable to their communities and culture. These are they who possess the capacity to provide the moral soundness and wisdom in judicial matters that is indispensable to any thriving culture. The sixth is Parmenas, defined as constant. The name is composed of a Greek preposition, *para*, typically meaning along side and is joined to the word *meno* meaning to abide, remain or stay. Para is the same preposition that is used to refer to the Holy Spirit, *paracletos* in Greek, as the comforter. The only thing that abides constant without regard to time and eternity is truth. This committee of seven was charged with the awesome responsibility of bringing abiding stability and truth to the distribution process and Parmenas' name reflects that. The seventh and last of the group is Nicolas which is derived mainly from two words. The first is *Nikos* (nee'-kos) and meaning a conquest, triumph or victory. The second is *Laos* (lay'-os) from which we get our word laity. Overall it is rather amazing to observe the extent to which the names of the committee members relate strongly to moral qualities and virtues that are both nobel and decent. From every indication it appears that the names of these seven men bear an embedded message. It is a message communicating the inevitable outcome of the committee's work was to be that of unequivocal success. These distinguished men were consistent in their ability to administer the goods justly, unwavering in their godly character, and victorious championing the cause of the afflicted and thwarting the attacks of the adversary. As a result of effectively meeting the challenge before them there was a great restoration of unity, trust, truth and the joy of celebration among the people of God.

Furthermore, the thing that is most notable about the names of these men is that all seven are of Greek origin. This readily suggests that every member of the committee was of the same ethnicity as that of the widows who were being slighted. That means the committee was unanimously stacked in favor of the Grecian Jews. Can you imagine what might have been the disposition of those who filed the complaint if the committee were composed of persons having the same ethnicity as those responsible for their ongoing unfair treatment? What are the chances that the Jews of Grecian descent would still feel slighted when future distributions had been completed? Moreover, if those of strictly Jewish heritage had been elected to the committee, what pressures might have been brought to bear in an effort to insure continuance of the favoritism toward the Jewish widows while slighting those who were Hellenist. To the contrary, since all of the committee members were Grecian, there would be no opportunity for justice to suffer because someone wanted to avoid being labeled a traitor or Grecian lover. Yes, justice would indeed prevail because above all else each member of the committee was full of the Spirit of God and wisdom.

Chapter 15

Racism and Preferential Treatment

For there is no respect of persons with God. ~ Romans 2:11

Right at the point when I thought that it was feasible to consider wrapping up my writing I caught one of those late night talk shows and there it was once again, the Affirmative Action dilemma. On this occasion there was some sentiment by a gentleman who seemed very sincere in his desire to see fairness in society across the board. His contention was that Affirmative Action was racism and that one type of racism is no better than another. He was nothing short of adamant that it (Affirmative Action) is just not right. Well, no doubt society is filled with people who espouse to racist precepts and practices. However, let us be careful to distinguish between those in our world who are racist and societal racism. Taking all factors into consideration, it would seem that when we speak of racist behavior or mentality (be it an individual racist or societal racism), what is reflected is not merely a negative disposition toward others. Racism is usually coupled with an inordinate desire to give substance to hatred that is otherwise confined to the mind and heart. That is to say, that racists and societal racism seek to inflict ill upon those who are the object of their hate, their fear and their ignorance. Once sought out and identified, all that is lacking is the opportunity for expression. When opportunity presents itself we find the manifestation of oppression, discrimination, dehumanization and public embarrassment. Yet these are merely the tip of the iceberg when considered against a backdrop of innumerable murders typified by tree lynching, burning, bludgeoning, dismembering and whatever else the mind of unregenerate men who are consumed with hate can fathom. There is absolutely nothing about racism that focuses on bringing about a more wholesome state for anything or anyone. It is a negative mindset, expends negative energy, utilizes destructive means and culminates in destruction. The distinction is drawn in that it is possible to live in a society with racists and yet not be victim to a society that is governed by racists. The latter would inevitably result in a reign of racism. Yes, there is an enormous difference between living with a few or even a multitude of people with warped minds versus living in a society where those same warped minds are the governing authority (or where the rules that govern a society are an expression of ideology of those who are racist). On the one hand there is the sporadic encounter, however frequent that might be, with those racist individuals in society. On the other hand there is an inescapable institutionalized racism with hatred, ill will and oppression permeating every venue of society.

Therefore I believe we have an obligation to make a distinction between laws that are designed to arrest racial injustices and that which is racists at its core. The former is intended to help those historically abused by both racists and racism. The latter does not seek to help, does no good and has no capacity for good. It is a detestable evil, an addiction to hatred! Any law that can be passed in an effort to paralyze it cannot in truth be labeled as racist or racism. Given that we were all solely under the full effect and influence of the kingdom of God, I would readily and whole heartedly agree that all of our rules and laws could be eradicated in favor of the judgment and justice of

God. My confidence is that justice would be true, unobstructed, impartial and immediate.

There is no respect of persons with God. The same cannot be said however, about men and women dressed in fine attire or judicial garb. Being human, they are subject to be tainted by numerous predispositions that can affect their ability to arrive at just conclusions. As a result, we find the admonition:

Have not the faith of our Lord Jesus Christ with respect of persons, for if there come unto your assembly a man with a gold ring, in fine apparel, and there come in also a poor man in vile raiment, and ye have respect to him that weareth the fine clothing, and say unto him, sit thou here in a good place; and say to the poor, stand thou there, or sit here under my footstool, are ye not then partial in yourselves, and are become judges with evil thoughts? (James 2:1)

Christians are held to a higher standard of life and with it the responsibility to treat all people with equality as it relates to human worth and dignity. Any type of preferential treatment, which is invariably based upon that which is superficial, must value one person at the expense of unjustly devaluing another. This valuation/devaluation paradox can be based on education, skin color, eye color or other physical traits, money, social standing, and the list goes on. Once again we should be reminded, *...the Lord seeth not as man seeth; for man looketh on the outward appearance....* (1 Samuel 16:7).

James, in his epistle, looks at preferential treatment and sees a violation of one of the greatest commandments; *Thou shalt love thy neighbor as thyself.* From this perspective he concludes that any respect of persons (giving value or worth to an individual above that which is given to another) is a transgression of the law and therefore sinful. Through the eyes of the divine we are all seen in the same light (or darkness as the case may be). Our worth is not a measure of physical appearance, socio-economic status, academic achievement, the cost of the clothes we wear, the size of the house we live in, or otherwise. You see, from God's vantage point we are all in the same boat. *For all have sinned and come short of the glory of God* (Romans 3:23). God loves us not because we are lovable (quite the contrary); He loves us because it is His nature to love and not because we are more valuable or lovable than "those folks" from the other side of the tracks.

But God who is rich in mercy, for his great love with which he loved us, even when we were dead in sins, hath |made us alive| together with Christ (by grace ye are saved) Ephesians (2:4-5).

The greatest potential for overcoming racial hatred, bigotry and the many other evils that plague us, is a relationship with the risen Savior Christ Jesus. That relationship can be established only by submitting ourselves to the *Master Plan* -- the greatest Affirmative Action plan ever implemented!

To wit, that God was in Christ reconciling the world unto himself, not imputing their trespasses unto them.... (II Corinthians 5:19). *The Lord is... longsuffering toward us, not willing that any should perish but that all should come to repentance* (II Peter 3:9). *For there is no respect of persons with God. For whosoever shall call upon the name of the Lord shall be saved* (Romans 2:11; 10:13).

Thou art weighed in the balances, and art found wanting
(Daniel 5:27)

Believe on the Lord Jesus Christ and thou shalt be saved,
and thine house (Acts 16:31)